Steam Memories On Shed: 1950's - 19

No. 93 NORTH EASTERN & Their Motive Power

DAVID DUNN

Copyright Book Law Publications 2016
ISBN 978-1-909625-62-4

INTRODUCTION

To finish off our review of the York group engine sheds, we take a look at Scarborough, Malton, and Whitby. All three depots were to disappear before steam was totally eliminated from the North Eastern Region but before that time, numerous photographers visited the sheds to capture the usual and unusual motive power, both resident and visitors alike.

Scarborough in particular had one photographer who appeared to have made it a mission to capture virtually every aspect of the depot and the motive power therein – Norman W.Skinner. Perhaps the Scarborough section of this album could be dedicated to Mr Skinner who was also very good with the camera.

Malton and Whitby were both small establishments but they too managed to pack in some large locomotives within the confines of their two-road shed buildings. We haven't counted the number of classes covered in this album but they are diverse and numerous so sit back and enjoy another helping of nostalgia.

As usual we thank the Armstrong Railway Photographic Trust for the use of images in this album.

David Dunn, Cramlington, June 2016

(cover) See page 70.

(previous page) The classic view of the northern end of Scarborough shed yard from Seamer Road on the glorious Saturday evening of 24th July 1954. Visiting motive power is being made ready for the return workings; tomorrow it'll all start again!   *R.F.Payne (ARPT)*.

Printed and bound by The Amadeus Press, Cleckheaton, West Yorkshire
First published in the United Kingdom by Book Law Publications, 382 Carlton Hill, Nottingham, NG4 1JA

A nice view of the straight shed on 18th July 1956 when it was fully intact with no buttress supports and a virtual full house. It looks like a summer evening with engines ready to back down to the station and return from whence they came. Amongst the throng here are B1, B16, D49, Stanier Class 5, Ivatt Class 4, BR Standard Cl.3, etc., etc., with nothing exotic to get excited about; identified are B1s Nos.61306 from Botanic Gardens, and 61017 BUSHBUCK which may have been from York. What a great view though from Seamer Road; undoubtedly it must have been amongst the most accessible – visually – engine sheds in the country.

R.F.Payne (ARPT).

It wasn't everyday that you saw an A5 on Scarborough shed so this specimen from Darlington was a bit of a treat for local enthusiasts. Unfortunately we have no date for the image either but we can perhaps find a period in the Fifties when the Pacific tank probably made the journey to the seaside town. During BR times No.69838 was allocated to Darlington from 1st January 1948 to 15th April 1951 (it had actually been at Darlington from 20th March 1939 but we can discount everything up to 3rd March 1949 when the locomotive became 69838) and then from 20th May 1951 to 19th June 1955. It's general condition is not exactly pristine so it must have been due for overhaul; the fact that it undertook three 'Generals' in that period doesn't really help either. It is summer because the train heating connecting hose has been removed, a normal summer routine at most depots. So there we have it its summer but in which year 49, 50, 51, 52 (before August), 53 or 54? The choice is yours unless you know the answer and in which case please contact us via the usual channels.

D.R.Dunn collection.

(opposite) For approximately six months of every year – April to September – during BR days, Scarborough was inundated with locomotives from all over the Eastern, North Eastern and Midland regions. Anything could and did turn up during those spring, and summer months on excursions and special workings. For the local enthusiasts it was something of a spotters' paradise. A typical example was this Stanier 8F *(top)* which had arrived on a special working from Dewsbury on 31st May 1958, and which was a recent acquisition by Mirfield shed from Wakefield. Although not the cleanest of locomotives (there is some irony somewhere when the headboard is perused), the eight-coupled Stanier was perhaps better than one of 56D's WD 2-8-0s being given the job depending where your loyalties lie. *(bottom)* Six years earlier the same photographer's camera captured Millhouses based Stanier Class 5 No.44986, with one of those self-weighing tenders, looking half decent on 28th June 1952.

both N.W.Skinner (ARPT).

4

On Sunday 13th July 1952 our photographer caught a couple of foreigners using the depot's 60ft turntable prior before setting back onto the yard. *(above)* Wakefield based Class 5 No.45201 fits comfortably on the device whilst *(below)* Huddersfield 'Crab' No.42861 has plenty of room and would perhaps require a bit of balancing for the manual turning process to be made easier. It's amazing that a shed such as Scarborough, where virtually all visiting engines (a hundred or more during any week in the summer season) required turning, never got the necessary aids fitted to the turntable. The engines might also visit the coaling stage, in the 'Crab's' case it appears to be a necessity. *both N.W.Skinner (ARPT)*.

Delicately balanced, York V2 No.60963 is halfway through the process on 21st November 1964. By now the shed was officially closed to everything but still locomotives came to turn and or stable, steam and diesel alike. No.60963 has plenty of coal in its tender so the absent of coalmen was not a problem; however I hope that someone was pushing at the rear of the locomotive. Why the stabilisers on the turntable? These were fitted to counteract any instability in the ground – the shed building was already suffering – which could cause great inconvenience to those turning the engines, and could in the worse instance cause a catastrophic capsize. Note the date 1/7/62 painted on the pit wall where the tracks join on the right side; this was probably the date of its last service when everything was checked and made good? Now, its one thing shifting six tons of coal on a long trip but pushing 144 tons of engine and tender was not quite in the remit!

N.W.Skinner (ARPT).

More visitors on the turntable! *(opposite, top)* Nameless 'Jubilee' No.45739, formerly ULSTER, wearing the latest accessory on its cabside, makes use of the device on a rather sunny 30th August 1966; this 6P came from Wakefield *(opposite, bottom)* On a rather damp day beforehand, sister No.45562 ALBERTA, also with cab stripes but from Farnley Junction, is in the same position whereas our intrepid cameraman has remained clear of the tracks. This aspect allows us to see the vandalism wrought on the empty and now derelict roundhouse; miraculously the clock was still working. Now, just take a look at that signal gantry!   *both N.W.Skinner (ARPT).*

Earlier that month – another sunny day too – on Wednesday 10th to be exact, the Wakefield 'Jubilee' was stabled on the old shed site alongside Stanier Cl.5 No.45277 from Llandudno Junction which had worked in on special 1Z10 from goodness knows where. Note that No.45739 had a nameplate on this date.   *N.W.Skinner (ARPT).*

Just arriving from the station on the last day of July 1965, Cl.5 No.45255 of Newton Heath, and BR Sulzer Type 2 D5161 from Thornaby, stand next to the roundhouse whilst waiting for the signal to go 'on shed' to turn and stable. Once steam was banished from Scarborough, the old shed site was vacated and diesel locomotives stabled in one or more of the terminal station platforms laid aside for the purpose. Of course, travel to the resort by train was not as popular as the decade wore on; by the early '70's only handfuls of excursion trains or specials were arriving. The holiday tastes of Britain were changing and British resorts falling out of favour to foreign destinations. *N.W.Skinner (ARPT).*

Yes another diesel! Brush Type 4 D1524 rests on the coaling road on 4th August 1963 after making history as the first of her class to visit Scarborough. This image has been used in our *D for Diesels* series but is worth a second outing simply because it illustrates the coaling stage situation as seen from the shed yard. The coal chutes consist two serving this road and a third located above a recessed road. The whole stage was bereft of a roof and the coalmen used the little hut provided for them on the coaling floor as a mess or refuge. When the roof disappeared is unknown but the stage does present a rather clean and austere appearance compared with most NE Region engine shed coaling stages which tended to resemble ramshackle-cum-derelict industrial buildings. Note the large water tank situated on Seamer Road and overlooking the whole structure. Coal wagons were propelled up a ramp which began its ascent opposite the north end of the engine shed. The maximum capacity was ten wagons which just fit on the coaling floor. Scarborough did not appear to specifically use tank engines as shed pilots in BR days and would utilise any available engine on the shed yard to shunt the coal stage so that it was possible to see a B16, WD, or a D49 running up the ramp to collect the empties and then repeating the exercise with a batch or two of full wagons. The shed had recently closed – 20th July – and the coaling facility was certainly now abolished even though steam locomotives were using the turntable, and the shed roads for stabling. It must be remembered that a servicing area, operational from June 1908 to September 1958, was located at Gallows Close and which had a 60ft turntable, coaling crane (hand-draulic), water column, and a 60ft pit for ash and clinker.

N.W.Skinner (ARPT).

Another ex-*DforD* image which has become useful for showing detail is this illustration of two English Electric Type 1s – D8062 and D8066 from Sheffield – utilising the coaling road/roundhouse yard entrance on Saturday 13th June 1964 after working in on an excursion. Anyway, the detail is really for the modelling fraternity who can see that the old coaling stage used recovered rail to form the frame of this coal chute (the other coal face employed what looked liked 8-inch, or similar, rolled steel joists – *see* next illustrations too). Further detail of the mechanism which allowed the coal barrows to connect and then be upended is not illustrated because it had been removed by this date but at least one tiny bit of realism can be presented.

N.W.Skinner (ARPT).

(opposite, top & bottom) These two September 1962 photographs show what we have just mentioned, along with the loaded 10-hundredweight capacity coaling barrows. The sunshine was not unusual at this time of the year and the holiday season was still in full swing as far as the coastal resorts were concerned, Scarborough included. Ivatt Class 2 No.46409 was another of those locomotives which had been built too late – or had steam been banished too soon – and so found little useful work anywhere. Scarborough was the recipient of this particular example which had spent its formative years at Goole. It came to 50E and spent more time in store than actually working. In this view we can see the chimney has a cover of sorts, though not the usual cloth job. It appears that a start has been made to paint the locomotive or clean so thoroughly it looks as though paint was applied – a commendable effort whichever medium was used. Was it ever finished? Did the 2-6-0 ever work again?

both N.W.Skinner (ARPT).

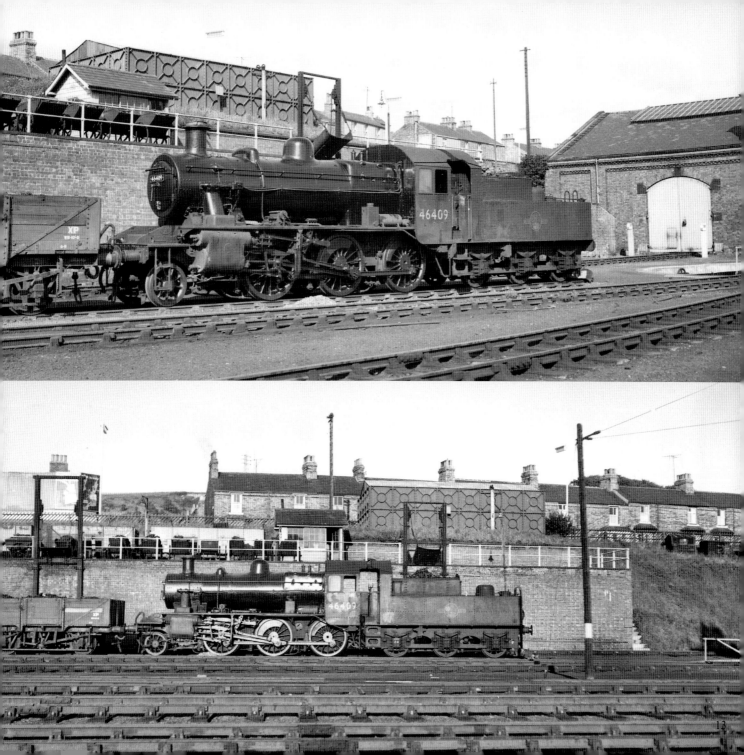

Some eight years earlier the westernmost coaling road had a semi-permanent resident in the shape of this former North Eastern clerestory bogie brake which has been utilised by the Chief Mechanical Engineer's Department and was employed as a Mess and Tool van when photographed on 4th April 1954. The date assumes the vehicle was stabled there during the winter but for what reason is unknown. Note the retro-fitted window in the centre of the bodyside just left of the centre double doors. Above, on the coaling floor are the neat regimented lines of barrows loaded with coal and waiting to serve the next locomotive requiring replenishment. *F.W.Hampson (ARPT).*

A near Christmas card scene at Scarborough on 20th January 1963; this was during the worst winter for decades which truly played havoc with virtually all forms of transport in the country. The railways were not immune and the diesel fleet on which BR had placed so much responsibility failed to battle through the weeks on end of severe cold. Steam locomotives which had been withdrawn and laid aside for scrapping were suddenly brought back into traffic. It was chaotic but for the observer an exciting time albeit very cold on the feet whilst waiting around for something to happen. There was not a lot happening at Scarborough shed on this Sunday morning, but traditionally that was a day when the railways took a short rest, re-grouped, and got ready for the next week. None of the locomotives here including three WD 2-8-0s, No.90045 nearest, and a solitary B16 No.61435 were going anywhere in the next twenty-four hours according to the attached 'Do Not Move' flags! The scene does look bleak and indeed it was with temperatures not lifting above freezing, snow refusing to melt, and not a lot moving about (just in case any of the wagons on the coaling stage fancied a stroll, the catch points were there to save the day). It was a time to stay indoors but that wasn't possible for many who had to work or at least try to work in the Arctic like conditions. Even children who normally made the best of the winter snowfall to enjoy themselves one way or another started to find the conditions monotonous and suddenly wresting on television from Scunthorpe baths, or wherever, hosted by Kent Walton got a whole new audience.

N.W.Skinner (ARPT).

Onward to the summer season! The inside of the engine shed on 22nd June 1963 with diesels having apparently taken over; EE Type 3 D6735 contrasts with the gas lighting hanging from the roof in front of the Co-Co. A Brush Type 2 hogs No.1 road.   *A.Ives (ARPT)*.

Mention of the diesel locomotives using the station for stabling in latter years leads us to this image which shows four of them using platform 7 on Sunday 27th June 1965. This was what sufficed as a shed for the majority of the diesels working into Scarborough. Meanwhile, the even bigger curse of steam locomotive enthusiasts crowd the other platforms in the station – the DMU was even pushing out the locomotive hauled trains and a new generation was to eventually rule the world! But who would have believed that in the final decade of steam? *N.W.Skinner (ARPT).*

Meanwhile back at the 'closed' depot just weeks later, on 4th August 1965, the usual suspects stable in the opened-out section of the shed. B1 No.61329 of Doncaster is nearest, 'Jubilee' No.45694 has shown up again from Wakefield, and a York B1 No.61337 makes up the trio. *N.W.Skinner (ARPT)*.

An undated image of the turntable pit, and its immediate surroundings: The 60ft appliance has been lifted out of its circular home by a breakdown crane – the temporary built-up 'fixed' track was erected to allow the crane to get right up to the table and then swing it round to a bogie bolster wagon or similar so that the table could be taken off to works for overhaul or cutting up. Its stabilisers have been left behind ready for the return or installation of another. Of course turntables were sometimes condemned and either a new one made, or a similar redundant device was appropriated from elsewhere. In Scarborough's case this writer does not know the full story of this table or when the event took place. However, the depot required a turntable for sure so one was got from somewhere assuming the original had failed its testing. Now, just to throw another spanner at you; Gallows Close servicing area closed for business in September 1958 and it had a 60ft turntable which would hardly be worn out. So, was that particular appliance transferred to Seamer Road shed? Note the clock is telling us its ten minutes to twelve and the sun is due south which tells us little about what time of year it is but the inclination indicates the sun is lower than during summertime so it could be early autumn. This unusual aspect affords us a view of the steel plates making up the coaling stage floor.

N.W.Skinner (ARPT).

The view over the fence on Saturday 15th September 1962 revealed York based B16/3 apparently in a state of semi-hibernation with what appears to be a cardboard box rather than the traditional hessian and tarp on the chimney. There could be lots of 'perhaps' about this engine's presence at Scarborough not least the fact that it isn't turned ready to work back home; perhaps it was going to work over the Whitby line; the engine is obviously 'dead' otherwise that box would be floating away on the hot air exhausting from the chimney; it had recently undergone a Casual Heavy overhaul (18th May to 28th June 1962) so was not in dire need of works attention – two months at York has certainly taken away the ex-works sheen – but it could have developed a mechanical defect requiring attention from fitters or boilersmiths; it would be two more years before it was condemned so it must have returned to traffic at some point. Here it was probably just stored as surplus like so many of York's charges at this time (see later). From this aspect it is possible to make out the nameboard on the signal box which is simply Gasworks.   *N.W.Skinner (ARPT).*

Going onto the yard on that same Saturday we come across another York B16/3, No.61434, on the same storage road which Scarborough used for engines awaiting works. Once again, this 4-6-0 is not prepared for any storage, its tender is full of ... well, something (quite a difference to the contents of 61448's tender). However, note that the cab windows, as per 61448, had been closed as was usual for locomotives entering storage or even withdrawal. This engine too had undergone a major overhaul earlier in the year so was not due for shopping. York's inability to clean its engines during this period really does stick out. It was of course the end of the summer timetable and many engines were not required for further service until the next major holiday period or even next summer. Don't forget the growing army of diesels which were pinching all the work and sending steam into situations like this. A good harsh winter would sort things out no doubt and indeed that was the case as the diesels fell by the wayside and stored steam everywhere was reactivated – temporarily though – to help keep the system running. The locomotive sandwiched between the two B16s was a WD 2-8-0 but we have no record of what it was but no doubt it had a 50A shedplate. So, what was inside the shed?   *N.W.Skinner (ARPT).*

(above left) Ex-LMS Class 4 No.42553 exits the roundhouse via the yard entrance on the morning of Saturday 5th September 1959. The York based 2-6-4T had just made use of the turntable located in the roundhouse because the yard table was incapacitated (is this the period when the table was 'out' as reported above?). Because so many former LMS locomotives were visiting and being allocated to Scarborough, one could be forgiven thinking it was an ex-LMS shed but it was purely North Eastern which by a series of events had found itself surrounded by things LMS. This Cl.4 tank had, since being put into traffic at Nottingham in the summer of 1936, led an interesting life after moving to Kentish Town in December 1939 to spend most of the war years in London before transferring to Newton Heath in July 1944. Then, in November 1946 it ventured into Yorkshire and never left the county until December 1961 when Darlington used it for its final year. *(right)* Seven years earlier, during the evening of 20th July 1952, Gresley V1 No.67677 was poised in the entrance to the roundhouse looking for a stall for the night; note the lone door where there should have been two! The Middlesbrough based tank eventually became a V3 in 1958 by which time it was based at Botanic Gardens. *both N.W.Skinner (ARPT).*

(above) Looking across the main line from the public lane near the gas works on 7th June 1959, we see ex-LMS 'Patriot' No.45504 ROYAL SIGNALS stabled on the nearest shed road after working in on an early train from York. The Bristol based 6P had been borrowed by 50A to head one of their time-tabled trains whilst the 4-6-0 was laying over prior to working a Newcastle-Bristol passenger service. *(below)* Making use of the turntable.

N.W.Skinner (ARPT).

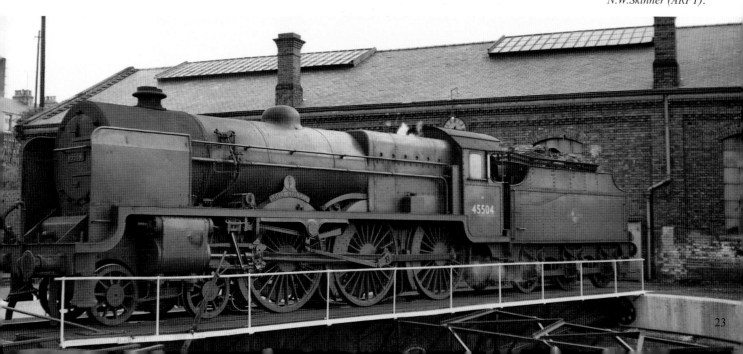

No, it's true! J11 No.64357 had worked into Scarborough and was being turned for its return journey back to Manchester on Sunday 19th July 1953. Gorton shed was still part of the Eastern Region in 1953 so the 0-6-0 still has the 39A shed plate. Which way the J11 brought its train would be fairly predictable but nevertheless, it is a commendable run out, and back, for the engine. It would be interesting to know where the footplatemen were from: York, or perhaps Mexborough men with a York pilot to Scarborough. Surely not Gorton men this far out! The Guard is sticking with the engine and its crew, no matter what.   *N.W.Skinner (ARPT).*

(opposite) Three A8, Nos.69867, 69877, and 69885 were stored in the roundhouse in June 1959. All of them had a cover over their chimneys, only one of which matched-up to the usual tarp and hessian. Still, they were somewhat better perhaps than a cardboard box.   *A.R.Thompson (ARPT).*

This Scarborough section of the album is becoming something of a tribute to photographer Norman W. Skinner so it would be gracious to include his first ever railway orientated photograph as a thanks for all the thousands of images he created for our pleasure over the years. The date is 12th April 1952 and the subject was Thompson B1 No.61010 of Botanic Gardens; the locomotive was three weeks out from a 'General' hence the semi-clean finish. Named WILDEBEESTE, the B1 unusually had no names fitted on return from Darlington. This may be accounted for the fact that a boiler change was made and the old but refurbished boiler from No.61131 had been fitted to our subject. Eventually No.61010 was reunited with its nameplates. Nevertheless, this image was already of historical value as soon as it was exposed. *N.W.Skinner (ARPT)*.

Turning for home! Hull Dairycoates K3 No.61857, coupled with a GN tender, makes a welcome return from 'shopping' on 8th August 1959.

N.W.Skinner (ARPT).

The view from the coal stage on a rather dull Monday 7th June 1965; track removed, windows broken, slates missing, doors left open, rubbish taking over! B1 No.61189 from Low Moor is pushed around the pit after working in from Bradford on 1Z11. Still the steam kept coming and would do for a few more summers. Note the coal in the tender which is plenty for the run home. Named SIR WILLIAM GRAY, the plate on this side has been removed whereas the right side plate was still in situ as photographic evidence from that same day, and same photographer reveals.

N.W.Skinner (ARPT).

Malton J27 No.65849 rests in the uncovered section of the shed on 15th May 1962 waiting for a job to take it back home. When 50F closed in April 1963, the J27 was transferred to York where it was promptly condemned and then sent to Darlington for breaking up. Once the 62/63 winter was out of the way the accelerating condemned and scrap movement really took off; even diesel locomotives were getting called to the scrapyard!

N.W.Skinner (ARPT).

D49 No.62745 THE HURWORTH rests on No.1 road on 29th November 1958. A resident of Scarborough since 17th August, this would be the 4-4-0s last shed before a trip to Darlington saw the engine condemned on 16th March 1959. *N.W.Skinner (ARPT).*

(opposite) J94 No.68046 stables in the roundhouse on 9th September 1961 and is utilising one of the shorter stalls. These two illustrations show the west wall of the shed which was built with an oblong plan shape rather than the usual square plan shape because of restrictions imposed by the local geography. Only fifteen stalls were laid, and two of those were next to useless (note the trolley stabled alongside) but the shed was used for all sorts of storage over the years. The saddletank was another of York's leftovers although its actual date of storage here is unknown. Eventually it was transferred to Darlington (7th October 1962) where it did find further employment. Condemned in June 1964, No.68046 was sold for scrap in the following August. *both N.W.Skinner (ARPT).*

Another Gorton based engine! This time it was K3 No.61809 which was stabled on the coaling stage wagon line beside the straight shed some weeks beforehand on Saturday 6th June 1953. The half decent 2-6-0 shows off its 39A shedplate and 370 reporting number. The engine was altogether a more suitable choice for a trip from Lancashire to the East coast of Yorkshire. *N.W.Skinner (ARPT).*

A rather mixed procession from the station arrives alongside the depot on 27th June 1959. However, this lot had been nowhere near Londesborough Road station. 'Flying Pig' No.43123, D49 No.62770 THE PUCKERRIDGE (it had transferred away from Scarborough just a fortnight beforehand), and B16 No.61469 had all just arrived at Scarborough shed from Selby and have got the signal to proceed on shed for servicing on this Saturday morning. The reason for the trio arriving from 50C is unknown but perhaps 50E was having some motive power problems and Selby was nominated to help out. Assuming Selby had a problem with perhaps their coaling plant it would hardly be worthwhile sending engines such a long way for topping up especially as Scarborough had enough to do on a summer Saturday looking after all its normal visitors. It may well have been a rehearsal for the forthcoming closure which took place in October but BR didn't really do rehearsals for such events. Does anyone have the answer? .

W.Skinner (ARPT).

33

STORAGE - It started more or less when the 62' summer timetable ceased! A2/3s Nos.60516, 60522 and 60515 are laid up inside Scarborough's remaining portion of covered engine shed on 15th September 1962. The usual reservations of storage were being made and just to make sure nobody fancied utilising one of the Pacifics for a passenger turn, the 'Do Not Move' flags have been slotted onto the lamp irons. Some of the engines stored at 50E would end up in Scotland, at Polmadie of all places, others would return to their place of origin for breaking up; STRAIGHT DEAL went to Aberdeen Ferryhill on 2nd December whilst SUN STREAM and HYCILLA were both condemned here on 12th November. TEHRAN joined them on the growing list of withdrawn motive power. It was a desperate time for steam traction but extremely interesting for us enthusiasts as every shed visit revealed a surprise or shock, and most works visits provided plenty of the latter! All three of the engines illustrated here were moved about the shed simply to protect the wheel bearings and at Scarborough it became policy to not just move the locomotives a couple of inches but to change them around the roads perhaps for the staff to have something to do more than anything else. Nos.60515, 60516, and 60518 did not actually go to Doncaster for scrapping until March or April 1963, so remained laid-up here. Peppercorn A2 No.60526 joined the Thompson trio after it too was condemned in November 62'.   *N.W.Skinner (ARPT).*

(opposite, top) Nos.60516 and 60518 are settled in on No.1 road on 6th October 1962 whilst on the same Saturday afternoon *(opposite, bottom)* a BR Standard Cl.5 hauls No.60526 off No.1 road to place the A2/3 on No.2 road with No.60522; note the mound of coal in the tender!

both N.W.Skinner (ARPT).

No.60522 and 60526, nameless, but prepared for storage, are pushed along No.2 road towards the shed where they will spend some of the winter.
N.W.Skinner (ARPT).

(opposite, top) No.60516 and 60522 inside the shed on 15th October 1962. *(below)* On 6th October, Nos.60522 and 60526 were sorted out in the yard prior to being pushed into the shed for the winter hibernation.
both N.W.Skinner (ARPT).

No.60518 buffered up to 60516 in November 1962. The placing of the stove is interesting; did someone have an inkling of the severity and duration of the winter just starting? But such precautions seemed futile as condemnations became the order of the day!

N.W.Skinner (ARPT).

(opposite, top) Nos.60512 and 60515 inside the shed during November 1962; the former also went to Scotland in December and was one of those working from 66A. *(opposite)* January 1963, before the snow arrived in Scarborough but when the cold still ruled, condemned No.60516 was placed on No.5 road with the chimney sacking removed. Was this the prelude to a temporary entry back into service or preparation for that one-way journey to Doncaster?   *both N.W.Skinner (ARPT).*

York based V2 No.60847 ST PETER'S SCHOOL presented something of a problem to the personnel at Scarborough when the roundhouse was chosen as the venue to store the big engine. The date was 3rd September 1962, a Monday, and the summer timetable appears to have ended hence the 'laying-off' of numerous steam locomotives. Only ten months beforehand No.60847 had received a 'general' at Darlington whereby separate cylinders were fitted along with a refurbished boiler, and a new Smiths speedometer. The chimney has been covered with a receptacle which appears to have been popular at 50E. However, the length of the locomotive has presented the real problem in that the turntable was not quite big enough for the 2-6-2 and it's tender. How long (no pun intended) this V2 remained here is unknown but it went back to work eventually, at York, and remained fairly active until June 1965 when the inevitable occurred. *N.W.Skinner (ARPT)*.

(opposite, top) No.60515 6th October 1962: chimney sacked, nameplates removed but otherwise ready for the road. One the BR Standard Cl.3 tanks, also redundant, takes shelter before moving on to perhaps warmer climes. *(bottom)* Immaculate No.60522 as received at Scarborough on 23rd June 1962, just a week after leaving Doncaster 'Plant'. *both N.W.Skinner (ARPT)*.

Nothing glamorous about this engine or its appearance! J39 No.64857 was in open storage at Scarborough on the last day of October 1959; sister 64861 is stabled behind. We are in the tidied-up and opened-out section of the shed next to the main line, with the brick wall and corrugated screening keeping the elements out of the remaining covered four road section of the shed. In the background is the open lobby with the notice boards and other information protected behind glass, for now. Back to the locomotive, it will be noted that the 0-6-0 carries not only a 50D shedplate but it still has Starbeck painted on the bufferbeam some six weeks or so after that particular depot ceased to exist. Officially Nos.64857 and 64861 left Starbeck on 13th September 1959 on transfer to York but it seems that 50A neither needed them nor wanted them and so sent them to Scarborough for storage, hence the 50D identification misnomer. No.64857 went to Thornaby on 22nd November 1959, followed on 13th December by No.64861; I'll lay odds that neither engine went near York before the move to 51L.

N.W.Skinner (ARPT).

A Few Standards: Class 3 tank No.82027 simmers on the shed yard on 18th May 1963. Scarborough's allocation was never very large; it entered the LNER with twenty-seven locomotives allocated but when BR came into being a quarter century later, only eleven engines were shedded. The decline continued throughout the BR period with just a few Standards remaining to the end. Of course, as we have seen, the depot became an excellent dumping ground for York's more glamorous steam clientele. *N.W.Skinner (ARPT).*

The ultimate in freight motive power. Wellingborough 9F No.92058 draws admiring crowds during its visit on 23rd July 1960. Having turned on Scarborough's 60ft table, the big engine takes on some water; perhaps a ton or two of coal wouldn't go amiss either because it's a fair old run to Wellingborough. The 2-10-0 was nearly five years old and would manage to stay operational for another seven years, quite remarkable for this class when the waste was considered. Up to this date this particular 9F was averaging 30,100 miles revenue service per annum; this little outing will certainly boost that average and indeed it did as 32,400 miles were logged for 1960. However, 1959 had seen 38,700 miles clocked up! As time wore on annual mileages declined, the new diesel locomotives began taking away the traffic which remained after the road transport industry had started to take advantage of the restrictions BR was saddled with by successive Governments. Waste was the order of the day!   *N.W.Skinner (ARPT)*.

(opposite) The two sides of THOMAS HARDY! 'Britannia' No.70034 visited Scarborough on Friday 1st September 1961 *(top)* and was still resident next morning. The Norwich based engine was looking rather smart which was no coincidence because it was just ex-works from Doncaster after heavy overhaul when this milometer was fitted. How the Pacific ended up in Scarborough on a Friday afternoon is anybody's guess but more than likely it was on a running-in turn from 36A, got to 50A for turning and then got seconded by York to do a trip to the seaside; the latter shed were notorious for such antics! *(bottom)* In this illustration we see the ER engine, with a minimum amount of coal but with plenty of steam, making a dash for it to get off shed.
    both N.W.Skinner (ARPT).

Another Brit! Looking about as far from 'ex-works' as it was possible to get, No.70003 JOHN BUNYAN from March shed rests on the shed yard on 15th July 1961. This engine will have worked in from York no doubt after arriving on the Colchester-Newcastle express; a NE Region Pacific (or diesel by this time) would have taken the express northwards allowing the 'Brit' to take up other duties for 50A before working back to Essex from York on the southbound Newcastle-Colchester the following day. Speculatively, was No.70034 on a similar duty? *N.W.Skinner (ARPT).*

Back to our favourite turntable. The date is 12th June 1954 and brand new BR Standard Cl.4 No.76036 has just run onto the table on this Saturday afternoon after arriving in Scarborough from York whilst taking part in running-in trials from Doncaster. The engine would not be going back to Doncaster until Monday morning so York will do with it what they will. Eventually, when 'put into traffic' the 2-6-0 will make its way to Neasden where it was initially allocated along with sisters 76035, and 76037 to 76044. Right! Anybody fancy a push?   *N.W.Skinner (ARPT).*

They didn't get much dirtier than this. BR Std. Class 5 No.75013 is turned, water, and coaled, ready for its return journey to where on 29th July 1964. Based at Bletchley, it seems to be stretching a point somewhat to have expected the 4-6-0 to have worked a special or anything from the south Midlands which was virtually in the Home Counties. More than likely the engine has worked to somewhere and the local shed has collared it to head an excursion to Scarborough. So, from virtually the furthest point in England to the sea geographically, this urchin has managed to work a day out at the seaside. When reallocated to Machynlleth on June 1965 No.75013 must have thought it was going on a personal tour of Britain and it nearly was except it all ended at Stoke-on-Trent in August 1967. Enough of the Standard, look what's flanking the engine; on the left is Wakefield 'Jubilee' No.45589 GWALIOR, whilst on the right is one of Doncaster's B1s, No.61360. However, the star of the show (and that is why this image is being used) is that little piece of brickwork still holding up the signal gantry, without flinching (see later for the explanation)!   *N.W.Skinner (ARPT).*

Now then, just look at that miniature plough! Scarborough's very own BR Std. Cl.3 No.77004 stands ready for action in fighting the elements during November 1962 (did somebody know of what was in store for the country as a whole?). Smart is the word which springs-to-mind and the 2-6-0 certainly looks that in a period when filth was the usual livery. Note that extra 50E shedplate on the bufferbeam; I'm still wondering what that extra personal touch is about. Transferred from York in November 1959, this engine stayed at 50E until the 'official' end and departed back to York in April 1963. Certainly a busy engine as regards sheds, No.77004 managed fifteen residencies during its twelve year existence, a class record. During the severe weather event of 1962-63, this useful engine excelled at helping out on services where diesels feared to tread. It left the shed for 50A complete with that snowplough; as for the shed plates, who knows? *N.W.Skinner (ARPT)*.

DEMOLITION!

Demolition of the eastern section of the shed had started by Saturday 19th September 1959 – the work apparently began immediately after the end of the summer timetable so as to cause the least inconvenience. Wagons have been placed inside the building to catch debris and detritus of the operation. The stout timber buttress with its even sturdier concrete foundation, had been doing its job of holding up this gable wall for a couple of years now – a similar structure was erected for the gable wall of the western four-road section of the shed – but that job was nearing its end and only the concrete foundation would remain to closure. Note the chalked message on the brick column warning all and sundry of the dangers of entering the shed. It's amazing how the B1 was left stabled on the brink of the shed entrance.   *N.W.Skinner (ARPT).*

Job completed! The now totally roofless shed on Sunday 8th November 1959 with a bevy of J39s, including Nos.64758 and 64904, stabled within. It appears that the east wall demolition had begun but was stopped because the signal gantry was actually incorporated within the fabric of the brickwork (eagle-eyed readers should have spotted the four bolts projecting inside the shed in the previous illustration; just beyond the first window opening); so, no easy solution there then! Note the rather ancient four-wheel carriage occupying the No.6 road, courtesy of York District Engineers. The line on the left was the main entrance to the shed yard, light engines usually coming from the station in groups, crossing from the Up main at Gasworks signal box, across the Down main and over onto this track to set back onto the shed yard. Regarding the J39s, these appear to be stored temporarily as none of the usual chimney covering has taken place. As, the origins of the two identified engines conflict with any pattern which normally accompanies these events; No.64758 had been at Neville Hill until 1st November 1959 but had then transferred to Thornaby of all places (yes it was possible to get to Teesside via Scarborough) so appears to be in limbo. No.64904 was a York engine and which transferred to Dairycoates on 22nd November 1959. Ironically that 0-6-0 was re-allocated to Scarborough the following year but only from 11th September to 9th October when it returned to Hull. So, was this a Sunday gathering of visitors which by some coincidence consisted four (perhaps more) J39s, with three of them trapped by a relic from the past? Please contact via the usual channels. Finally on this one, where was all that timber on the surviving roof destined besides downwards!?

N.W.Skinner (ARPT). 51

Another classic view from Seamer Road showing the remaining section of straight shed on Monday 11th June 1962. The shed is quite full at what is probably evening time and it may well have been a Bank Holiday judging by the number of 'foreign' visitors. Amongst the throng is A1 No.60146, there are B1s, B16s, a couple of Stanier Cl.5s, an EE Type 4 diesel, and a least two Brush Type 2 diesels. Note the 'spotters' staying within the boundaries of the law and awaiting the gradual movements of locomotives from shed to station whereby everything would run to a slick and well tried departure routine without – hopefully – any hiccups. Again, those of you with eagle eyes or magnifying glasses will have noted the surviving section of shed wall still attached to that signal gantry. Scarborough had one more year like this before 'closure' and then demolition of the remaining four-road section of shed but it would be another four years before the spotters didn't bother to turn-up here anymore. *N.W.Skinner (ARPT).*

(above) Looking like one of those cut-away illustrations which became so popular to explain everything from aircraft to submarines, the long disused shed has succumbed at last. The date is 3rd April 1966. That it lasted this long is unbelievable. *(below)* A week later and progress has been made with the roof, the last vestiges now looking totally unsafe and ready to meet the ground. *both N.W.Skinner (ARPT)*.

By 24th April *(opposite, top)* the demolition contractors had made excellent progress and the yard should be ready for the summer seasonal traffic. Meanwhile that signal gantry clings onto the remaining brickwork of the east wall. *(opposite, bottom)* On Sunday 1st May the final section of the office block is ready for pulling down.

both N.W.Skinner (ARPT).

(this page) The view inside the roundhouse on 24th June 1966 with track lifted and the stall pits along with the turntable pit filled in with rubble from the straight shed. The date of its demolition is unknown but it wasn't too far off. Now does anyone know when that gantry was removed, along with its brick support?

N.W.Skinner (ARPT).

The east end of Malton shed circa 1962 with BR Standard Cl.2 No.82029 and a sister engine – probably 82028 – resting between duties. Their normal sphere of operations took them on passenger workings to Whitby, along with weekend trips to Scarborough and occasional goods workings. The original allocation of engines from this class to the North Eastern Region was for ten engines – 82020 to 82029 – but in the event only the last four of the building batch actually found their way to the region. Two went to the LMR whilst the other four went to the Southern, the latter region being the eventual destination for the NER quartet too but not before the NE Region had tried desperately to find appropriate work for them. Of the four, three worked from Malton: No.82027 from September 1958 to June 1960, then from December 1962 to April 1963; No.82028 from September 1961 to April 1963; and No.82029 from September 1958 to June 1960 and from September 1961 to April 1963. By September 1963 all three, along with No.82026 (the one that never came to Malton), were on the Southern. Malton shed had closed on Monday 15th April 1963 although its charges had left the shed on the day beforehand.

K.H.Cockerill (ARPT).

The other end of the shed in July 1960, complete with doors! A recent acquisition from York was this Stanier Cl.4 tank No.42477 which spent eighteen months at Malton along with younger sister No.42639. Both came from York and they moved on to Darlington together in time for Christmas 1961. They went their separate ways after that, our subject went to Chester whereas the young one went to Wakefield from where it was withdrawn in September 1964. No.42477 lasted until June 1965 and was a year and a bit short of achieving the 30 years design life. However, it had certainly been around from starting work at Patricroft in January 1937, it went to Swansea, then Polmadie via Stafford, back to Manchester then off to Yorkshire with Leeds in the mix too.

Maurice Burns. 57

The ramshackle but perfectly adequate coaling platform complete with its own fixed crane mounted on a concrete plinth. We are lucky in that the cameraman has chosen a moment in time when the coalman can be seen demonstrating the method of filling the tubs direct from the wagons with minimum effort. The crane is fired up ready to perform for the next customer but there are only four tubs on the stage note. The stage itself is one of those marvellous contraptions which evolve from laying a couple of old sleepers on the ground, followed by more until a required height and size is met whereby sheets of steel are introduced to make the job of pushing the tubs around the stage much easier. The first coaling crane was installed in 1870 and may well have this little beauty; recognised as Outdoor Machinery, the crane and its boiler will had had History Cards on which every detail of repair, change and overhaul would have been logged, not to mention make, type and age of model (has anyone got the originals or access to?). The shed was just out of frame to the right whilst the turntable was located to the left. The recently painted hut may well have been the time office, shed foreman's abode, and the enginemen's lobby but it could also have been the coalmen's mess room, up-to-date records are sadly lacking perhaps local knowledge would let us know via the usual channels. The date of this image was 15th July 1961 and the depot had nearly two years of operations ahead of it before closure.   *N.W.Skinner (ARPT).*

(opposite, top) The shed as viewed from the station's Up platform at an unknown date in the mid to late 1950s. Turned ready to head home, A8 No.69867 was a visitor from Scarborough but the J27s were residents, No.65849 having been so since the end of January 1955 and remaining at Malton until the penultimate day, 14th April 1963. No.65829, hiding inside the shed, had also been received by 50F on 23rd January 1955 but was condemned on 3rd July 1959 after arrival at Darlington for overhaul. The A8 had transferred to 50E at the end of May 1955 from Botanic Gardens and yes, it had been at Scarborough from 1952 until January 1955 but had left for Hull on the 9th. Therefore, we can only surmise that the date of the image is post May 1955 and before July 1959. Of yes, as you can see it is also summer with plenty of foliage on the trees and some rain clouds developing above Malton! *J.W.Armstrong (ARPT). (opposite, bottom)* A further aspect of the shed on another day of changeable weather: It is 4th April 1954, a Sunday afternoon, with G5 No.67308 from Pickering stabled at the west end of the shed. On the right are a couple of huts making up the Boilersmiths department whilst halfway down the building on the north wall was the fitters rather cramped premises. Beyond the signal are the tool vans for those little problematic events out on the line when locomotives and or rolling stock decide to step off the rails. Long before the G5 transferred to Pickering in February 1953, it had done a couple of stints at Malton; it came from Starbeck on 30th June 1939, then went to Pickering on 2nd October, and returned to Malton three weeks later on 23rd October 1939 whence it remained until moving to Whitby on 28th March 1942. Pickering would prove to be its final posting and on 22nd November 1955 it was condemned and later cut up at Darlington.   *F.W.Hampson (ARPT).*

These two vehicles made up the Malton Breakdown Train on 4th April 1954. Only a section of Tool Van No.DE 901604 is showing but we can make out to whom the van belongs. The other piece of stock must have been the riding van and it too is marked Loco Dept Malton but has no other identification visible. Nevertheless the vintage is unquestionable although it has been altered somewhat internally for its role with the motive power people and has two stoves installed – for heat and cooking? Some nine years were to elapse before the shed closed so the roof cladding seen here was to suffice until then because no new covering was ever fitted. The mixture of corrugated iron on the vents, and bitumen rolls on the main portion of the roof make interesting companions. *F.W.Hampson (ARPT).*

J39 No.64928 stands outside the west end of the shed in 1961. Note that the doors and the girder over the doorway have been painted. By now such an event was usually a prelude to impending closure but Malton shed benefited from the refurbishment by more than a year. Nevertheless, the painting appears to be a waste of money when it is considered that for much of the post-war period not a lick of paint was applied to any part of the shed. Oh yes, the J39 had been a resident of Malton since 26th October 1952; it was just about to be condemned. *A.R.Thompson (ARPT).* 61

An interior view of Malton on 30th July 1955 with resident A8 No.69877 being highlighted! Throughout the LNER period Malton had maintained an average allocation of approximately a dozen locomotives although at Grouping some eighteen engines represented by eight different classes were shedded there. Of the large ex-NER tanks, Class A6, and A7 usually had one representative. In BR days the A8 class began to appear simply because BR Standard types were ousting them from their traditional haunts although one or two had been allocated in the latter LNER period (No.1501/69880 from 5th September 1940 to 5th March 1942). This example did two stints at Malton – 7th June 1953 to 21st January 1956 and 3rd March to 15th September 1957 – so we see the big tank on its first residency. Others which came in BR days were: 69861 – 3rd June 1956 to 20th June 1960 when it was condemned; 69886 – 16th February 1958 to 21st June 1960 when it too was condemned; 69890 – 3rd June 1957 to 13th January 1958, which was the shortest period of allocation but one which saw the engine condemned when it went for overhaul at Darlington. So, from mid-1957 until mid-1960 Malton had two of the class allocated. Of course, when they went the BR Standards came and that is where we came in. *C.J.B.Sanderson (ARPT).*

50G - WHITBY

Looking rather busy for the time of year, this is Whitby engine shed and environs on Thursday 3rd April 1958. Identified locomotives include BR Standard Cl.3 No.77004 with another of the class – Nos.77012 and 77013 were also residents – near the shed. B1 No.61086 is a visitor from Neville Hill whilst A8 No.69886 is a visitor from Malton. Exactly one year and three days from now Whitby shed would close and its small allocation of just five locomotives would disperse to other NE Region depots. Although alterations did occur over the 110 year life of the shed, the somewhat cramped site did not allow for any modern aids to be installed although the LNER North Eastern Area and BR NE Region in turn, seemed somewhat opposed to modernisation. At least Whitby got a coaling crane.

F.W.Hampson (ARPT).

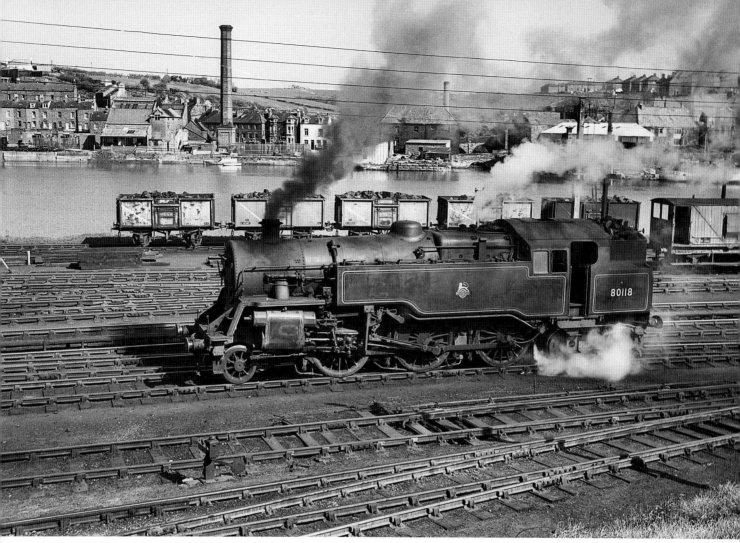

One thing Whitby was blessed with during its final years of operation was modern motive power and the BR Standard Class 4 tank was a superb locomotive for the requirements of the shed. Compared with the ancient and by now rickety A8s, the Standards certainly were a treat for the enginemen. This is No.80118 near the shed on 3rd May 1958 with the evening sun illuminating the scene. 50G had four of these 2-6-4T – Nos.80117, 80018, 80119, and 80120 – allocated from new and delivered from May to July 1955. No.80116 was actually the forerunner arriving at Whitby on 15th May 1955 but it had been allocated to York for a few days beforehand so didn't count as new! All five departed for pastures anew in Leeds on 8th June 1958, swapped for two former LMS Cl.4 tanks from Scarborough for the final months. The five 16-ton mineral wagons seemingly skirting the River Esk are the next lot of loaded wagons for the shed's coal stage which could handle five wagons at a time with little room to spare (*see* also previous illustration).

F.W.Hampson (ARPT).

No.80116 shortly after arrival from York in May 1955; already a 50G shedplate has been fitted whilst A8 No.69861 looks on from the shed entrance. The Pacific tank would linger on at Whitby until June of the following year when it transferred to Malton. Shortly afterwards it entered Darlington shops for a Casual Heavy overhaul; followed in early 1958 by a 'General' which would see it through to withdrawal in June 1960. Whitby shed had been well served by the A8 tanks over the years with no less than fifteen of them being allocated over the years from 1933 to near the end. Their smaller sisters the A6 had also been in residence for much of the LNER period and seven of those could be reckoned with too. *J.W.Armstrong (ARPT).* 65

Mention earlier of the cramped conditions at Whitby can be gathered from this image which illustrates some of the ancillary buildings (huts and sheds albeit substantial, and brick and stone built) used as stores (with the hipped roof), mess room (nearest with the flat roof), and the coal stage landing. The corrugated iron clad building on stilts overlooking everything is a private enterprise, one of many, on Windsor Terrace located above the depot.

J.W.Armstrong (ARPT).

A general view of the shed and its small yard on a rather sunny Sunday morning 4th April 1954 (the LNER's boast about their side of the country being the drier side seems to have to substance to the claim) with a couple of old-timers stabled. Inside the shed is long-time resident G5 No.67302 and being fiddled with in the yard is A8 No.69858 which was soon to leave the shed for Neville Hill with nothing coming in to replace it. When BR came into being, Whitby maintained a dozen locomotives made up of small and large tank engines (G5[5], A6[1] and A8[3]), and those versatile 0-6-0 tender engines (J24 [3]). Even up to June 1958 the numbers were reasonable and little changed at eleven – with 1 A8, 1 J25, 1 ex-LMS Cl.4, 3 BR Cl.3 2-6-0, five BR Cl.4 2-6-4T. The arrival of the diesel multiple unit was the one factor which put the final nails in Whitby's coffin (I'm not even thinking about a link with Bram Stoker). Modern motive power or not, the DMUs were nothing if not convenient, clean, etc., etc., etc. And, it meant that locations such as the shed here could be given up, and even sold off. Note the clutter on the coaling stage, and the huts on the highway above the shed – a modelling project? Especially if space was at a premium!

F.W.Hampson (ARPT).

Further detail for modellers on 4th April 1954; note the modern flat roofed brick building, the stone-built original with the hipped roof and attached to the shed, and that grounded wagon body between them. Not forgetting that the passenger station was just beyond the northern end of the shed, opposite the goods warehouse. Not wishing to push any readers into modelling any aspect of Whitby, those properties on Windsor Terrace look challenging with no two the same! Oh and don't forget the engine pits outside the shed. Now have you seen that wall bracket holding the gas lamp on the corner of the shed? Interesting! Whitby had a set of sheerlegs inside the shed at the other end of the building on this near road.   *F.W.Hampson (ARPT).*

Moving down the yard towards Bog Hall signal box on that Sunday morning in April 1954, we come across G5 No.67240 basking in the sun. This 0-4-4T had spent most of its life working in west Yorkshire but had now left behind the woollen mills, spa towns, and general industrial grime to end its days by the coast. However, it didn't quite work out like that. Transferred from Neville Hill to Whitby on 19th July 1953, the little tank was called to Malton at the end of November 1955 and was condemned six months later. It was good while it lasted! Behind we can see the shed's pride and joy, the steam crane used for coaling the engines. Very much like the Malton crane, this had been working here for many years and was equipped with wheels, rather than being fixed, to enable the appliance to work up and down the line of coal wagons because there was little room for shifting empty wagons so they remained in situ once the first couple had been emptied. Once all of them were empty the whole lot were changed in one action by the shunter of the day. The coalmen still had to fill the tubs though but these were then hoisted onto the stage to await customers. Once a locomotive was alongside the crane then went into its next operation lifting the tubs off the stage and over the waiting bunkers where they were tipped. The turntable at Whitby, a 50ft diameter hand powered affair, was located on the opposite side of the main line, just south of the level crossing next to Bog Hall box; a pit and water column complimented the facilities there.

F.W.Hampson (ARPT).

A nostalgic scene from 1952 with no less than three visiting D49s illustrated; a couple of A8s, a G5 and a J25 complete the line-up. Whitby once had its own D49 during the months leading up to World War II; No.255 (62742) THE BRAES OF DERWENT was allocated from 1st July to 11th September 1939 but returned to York at the end of the summer timetable (and normality). Other identified locomotives include J25 No.65663 and G5 No.67302, both residents, A8 No.69867 from Scarborough. Now look at some of that carriage stock; it is nearly as old as the buildings on the headland on the

other side of the river. *J.W.Armstrong (ARPT).*

A pair of J25s headed by York's No.65656 stable away from the shed in May 1955; note that the A8 has been well catered for by the coaling gang.

J.W.Armstrong (ARPT).

Yes, I think I'll claim this one! One of the older hands at Whitby poses with the shed's latest acquisition in May 1955 as resident A8 No.69865 looks on from inside the shed. More interesting stock occupies the carriage siding. *J.W.Armstrong (ARPT).*